KRAKEN

APEX

BY ARNOLD RINGSTAD

WWW.APEXEDITIONS.COM

Apex is distributed by North Star Editions:
sales@northstareditions.com | 888-417-0195

Produced for Apex by Red Line Editorial.

Photographs ©: Shutterstock Images, cover, 1, 4–5, 6–7, 8–9, 10–11, 12, 13, 14–15, 20–21, 26; iStockphoto, 16–17, 18–19, 27, 29; Christian Darkin/Science Source, 22–23; Science Source, 24–25

Library of Congress Control Number: 2020952929

ISBN
978-1-63738-021-5 (hardcover)
978-1-63738-057-4 (paperback)
978-1-63738-126-7 (ebook pdf)
978-1-63738-093-2 (hosted ebook)

Printed in the United States of America
Mankato, MN
082021

NOTE TO PARENTS AND EDUCATORS

Apex books are designed to build literacy skills in striving readers. Exciting, high-interest content attracts and holds readers' attention. The text is carefully leveled to allow students to achieve success quickly. Additional features, such as bolded glossary words for difficult terms, help build comprehension.

TABLE OF CONTENTS

CHAPTER 1

TERROR AT SEA 5

CHAPTER 2

THE KRAKEN'S HOME 11

CHAPTER 3

THE KRAKEN IN ACTION 17

CHAPTER 4

FROM LEGENDS TO SCIENCE 23

Comprehension Questions • 28
Glossary • 30
To Learn More • 31
About the Author • 31
Index • 32

TERROR AT SEA

The fishermen haul in their heavy nets. Suddenly, a dark shape moves under the boats. It's the kraken!

The kraken is said to lurk deep in the ocean.

According to legends, the kraken can pull any ship underwater.

Huge **tentacles** shoot up out of the water. They grab one of the boats. They drag it under the waves. The other fishermen are terrified. They try to escape.

A SIGN OF THE KRAKEN

In **legends**, good fishing is a sign the kraken is nearby. The creature scares fish into coming up to the water's surface.

The kraken slips back underwater. But it makes a **whirlpool.** One boat swirls down with the beast. The other boats get home safe.

It is hard for ships to get away from a whirlpool's swirling water.

Whirlpools appear in legends of several different monsters.

CHAPTER 2

THE KRAKEN'S HOME

The kraken is a **legendary** beast. It is said to live in the northern Atlantic Ocean. These waters are between Norway and Greenland.

The kraken is said to live in cold waters near the coast of Norway.

Sailors brought stories back to shore. They told of a huge beast with many arms.

Long ago, people in Norway used long boats to travel and fish.

Cod is one of the top kinds of fish caught in Norway.

PEOPLE OF THE SEA

Norway has a long coastline. Its people sailed to **distant** lands. They fished for food. The sea was important to them. This is clear in their legends, including tales of the kraken.

In some stories, the kraken can control the weather.

Sailors said the beast lived deep underwater. But sometimes it came up to the surface. It attacked boats. Then it sank back down.

Some stories say the kraken can eat a ship's entire crew.

CHAPTER 3

THE KRAKEN IN ACTION

A Scandinavian writer described the kraken in 1755. He gathered tales about the beast. He shared what he learned.

Some illustrations show the kraken grabbing boats.

The kraken looks similar to an octopus.

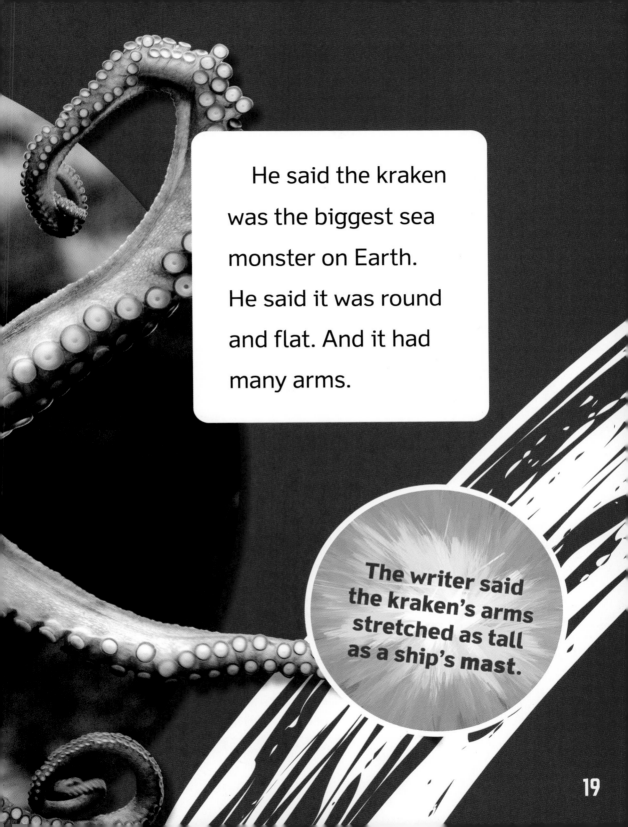

He said the kraken was the biggest sea monster on Earth. He said it was round and flat. And it had many arms.

The writer said the kraken's arms stretched as tall as a ship's mast.

The writer explained how the kraken hunted. He said its poop floated on the water. The smell **attracted** many fish. The kraken came up to eat them.

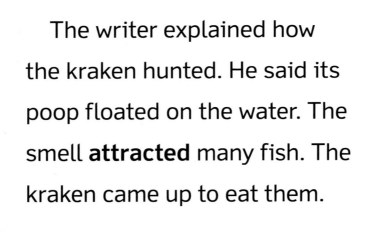

One Greek myth tells of a sea monster that lived in a whirlpool.

The kraken appears in many books, movies, and TV shows.

ANOTHER MONSTER

The kraken is similar to a Greek monster called Scylla. This monster has six heads. It sits on the coast. It eats sailors who come too close.

CHAPTER 4

FROM LEGENDS TO SCIENCE

In the 1850s, scientists began learning more about the giant squid. They realized the kraken might be based on this animal.

Giant squid hunt many animals, including fish, jellyfish, and other squid.

Giant squid sometimes wash up on beaches. This helps people learn about them.

24

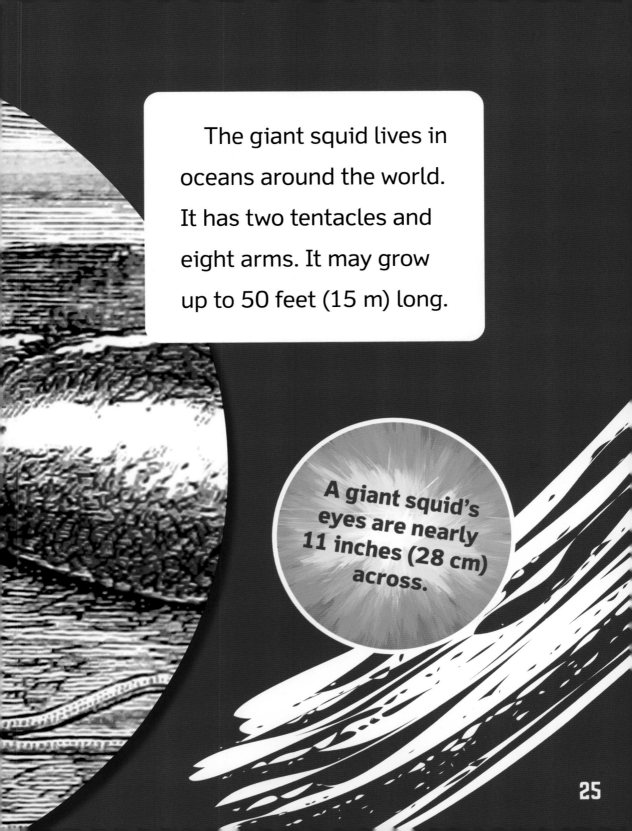

The giant squid lives in oceans around the world. It has two tentacles and eight arms. It may grow up to 50 feet (15 m) long.

A giant squid's eyes are nearly 11 inches (28 cm) across.

Long ago, sailors could have seen giant squid. They could have used tales of the kraken to explain what they saw.

The arms of a squid are covered in suction cups that can grab and hold things.

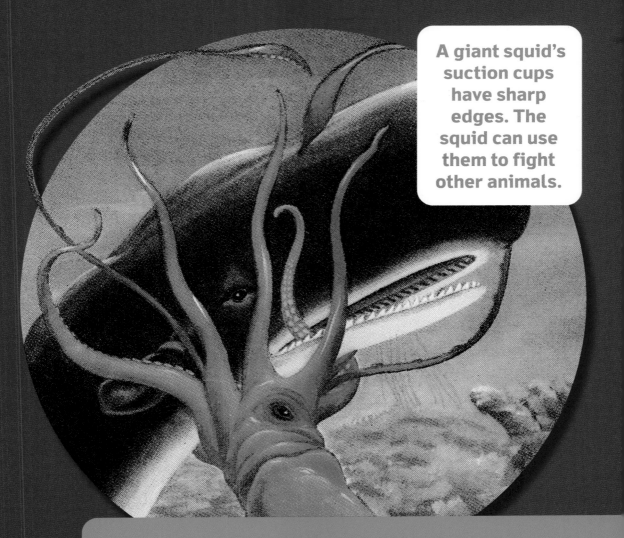

A giant squid's suction cups have sharp edges. The squid can use them to fight other animals.

ANOTHER BIG SQUID

The colossal squid may be even bigger than the giant squid. But it didn't **inspire** the kraken. It lives in a different part of the world. It is found only in the waters near Antarctica.

COMPREHENSION QUESTIONS

Write your answers on a separate piece of paper.

1. Write a paragraph telling the main ideas of Chapter 2.

2. Why do you think people tell so many legends that involve the ocean? Do those stories have anything in common?

3. According to legends, what does the kraken eat?

    A. squid

    B. fish

    C. whirlpools

4. Why do people think the giant squid inspired stories of the kraken?

    A. Both creatures are real animals.

    B. Both creatures live near Antarctica.

    C. Both creatures live in the Atlantic Ocean.

5. What does **described** mean in this book?

*A Scandinavian writer **described** the kraken in 1755. He gathered tales about the beast.*

    A. told what something was like

    B. saw something in real life

    C. took a long trip

6. What does **surface** mean in this book?

*Sailors said the beast lived deep underwater. But sometimes it came up to the **surface**.*

    A. the bottom of the ocean

    B. the top of the water

    C. the floor of a building

Answer key on page 32.

GLOSSARY

attracted
Made something come closer.

distant
Far away.

inspire
To start or give the idea for something.

legendary
Coming from popular stories told in the past.

legends
Famous stories about people, creatures, or events, often based on facts but sometimes not completely true.

mast
A tall post that holds a ship's sail.

Scandinavian
Coming from an area in northern Europe that includes the countries of Norway, Sweden, Denmark, Iceland, and Finland.

tentacles
The flexible limbs of animals such as squid.

whirlpool
An area of water that swirls downward.

TO LEARN MORE

BOOKS

Abdo, Kenny. *Cryptids*. Minneapolis: Abdo Publishing, 2020.

Goddu, Krystyna Poray. *Sea Monsters: From Kraken to Nessie*. Minneapolis: Lerner Publications, 2017.

Polinsky, Paige V. *Giant Squid: Mysterious Monster of the Deep*. Minneapolis: Abdo Publishing, 2017.

ONLINE RESOURCES

Visit **www.apexeditions.com** to find links and resources related to this title.

ABOUT THE AUTHOR

Arnold Ringstad lives in Minnesota with his wife and their cat. He enjoys reading about legendary beasts and the history behind them.

INDEX

A
Antarctica, 27
arms, 12, 19, 25
Atlantic Ocean, 11

B
boats, 5, 7–8, 14

C
colossal squid, 27

F
fish, 7, 20
fishing, 7, 13

G
giant squid, 23,
    25–27
Greenland, 11

H
hunting, 20

M
monsters, 9, 19, 21

N
Norway, 11, 13

S
sailors, 12, 14, 21,
    26
Scandinavian, 17
scientists, 23
Scylla, 21
ship, 15, 19

W
whirlpools, 8–9

Answer Key:
1. Answers will vary; **2.** Answers will vary; **3.** B; **4.** C; **5.** A; **6.** B